The Monster Book of ABC Sounds

To Tom, Tom, Joe,
Caroline & Tom

PUFFIN PIED PIPER BOOKS
Published by the Penguin Group
Penguin Books USA Inc., 375 Hudson Street, New York, New York 10014, U.S.A.
Penguin Books Ltd, 27 Wrights Lane, London W8 5TZ, England
Penguin Books Australia Ltd, Ringwood, Victoria, Australia
Penguin Books Canada Ltd, 10 Alcorn Avenue, Toronto, Ontario, Canada M4V 3B2
Penguin Books (N.Z.) Ltd, 182–190 Wairau Road, Auckland 10, New Zealand
Penguin Books Ltd, Registered Offices: Harmondsworth, Middlesex, England

First published in hardcover in the United States 1991 by
Dial Books for Young Readers
A Division of Penguin Books USA Inc.

Created and produced by
David Bennett Books Ltd.,
St Albans, England
Text copyright © 1991 by David Bennett Books Ltd.
Pictures copyright © 1991 by Alan Snow
All rights reserved
Library of Congress Catalog Card Number: 90-39384
Printed in Hong Kong
First Puffin Pied Piper Printing 1994
ISBN 0-14-055268-5
1 3 5 7 9 10 8 6 4 2

A Pied Piper Book is a registered trademark of
Dial Books for Young Readers, A Division of Penguin Books USA Inc.,
® TM 1,163,686 and ® TM 1,054,312.

THE MONSTER BOOK OF ABC SOUNDS
is also available in hardcover from
Dial Books for Young Readers.

The Monster Book of ABC Sounds

by

Alan Snow

A Puffin Pied Piper

The hide-and-seek game
is about to begin....

Bb

A monster pops out
from behind a small door,

Boo!

Cc

while three cunning rats
sneak a look 'neath the floor.

Cooeee!

Ee

Two more go upstairs and are in for a shock.

Ff

While one monster slips
in the chase and gets wet,

Hh

This ticklish young monster
is found by his feet.

Jj

One rather large monster
is anxious to play.

Jingle   Jangle

K k

Another poor monster splashes down and away.

Three monsters are found
by the sound of their song...

Mm

And this one finds honey,
which doesn't last long.

Nn

A very bold monster
zooms down just for kicks.

Neeeaaaw!

Oo

He flies upside down
and does other brave tricks.

P p

One of the monsters
runs right out of luck.

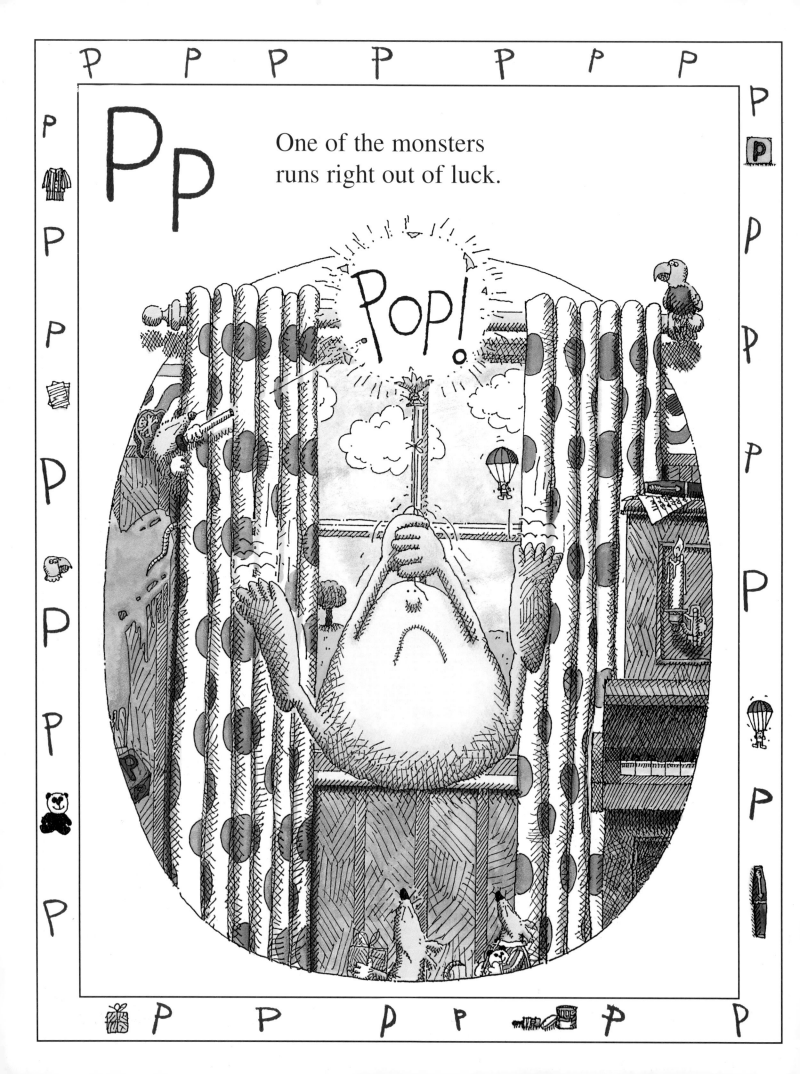

POP!

Another silly monster
pretends he's a duck.

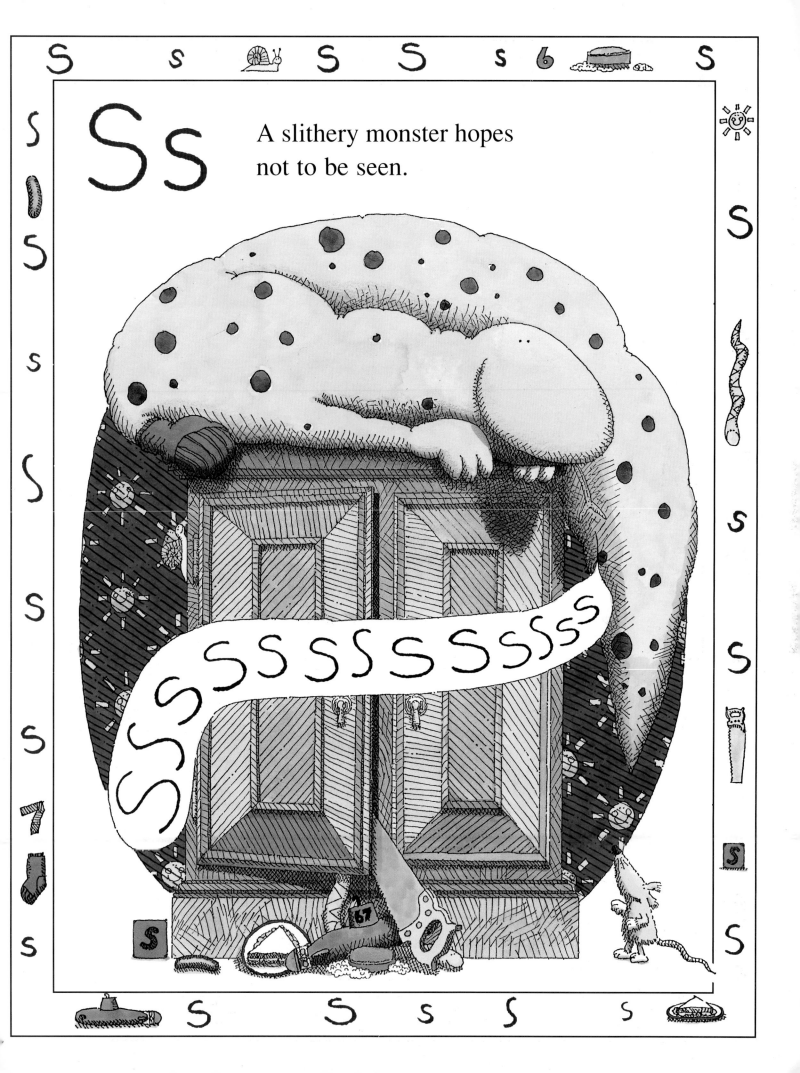

Ss

A slithery monster hopes not to be seen.

Tt

This monster is gasping
with hunger and thirst.

He goes to the cabinet,
but rats got there first.

V v

"I bet you can't catch me!"
is this monster's boast.

Vrrrooom!

Ww

"That's easy," the rat laughs.
"You're last past the post!"

Wheeeeee

Xx

The game is now over and wasn't it great?

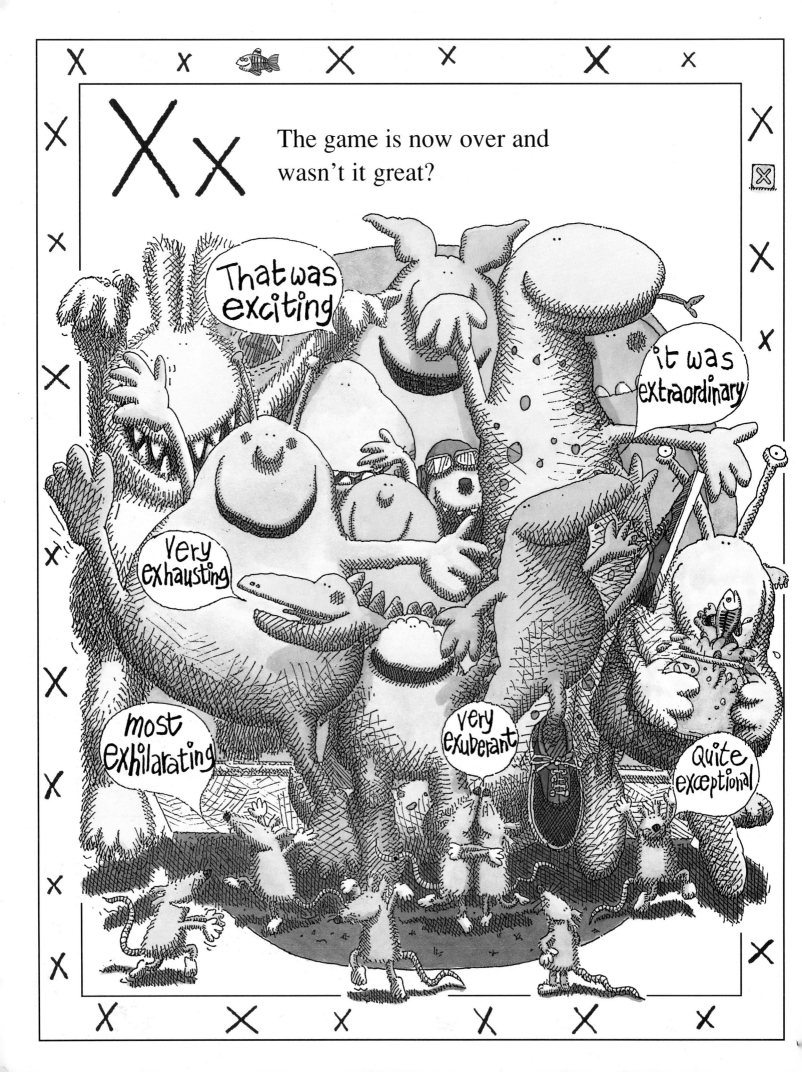

But it's bedtime for those
who have stayed up so late.

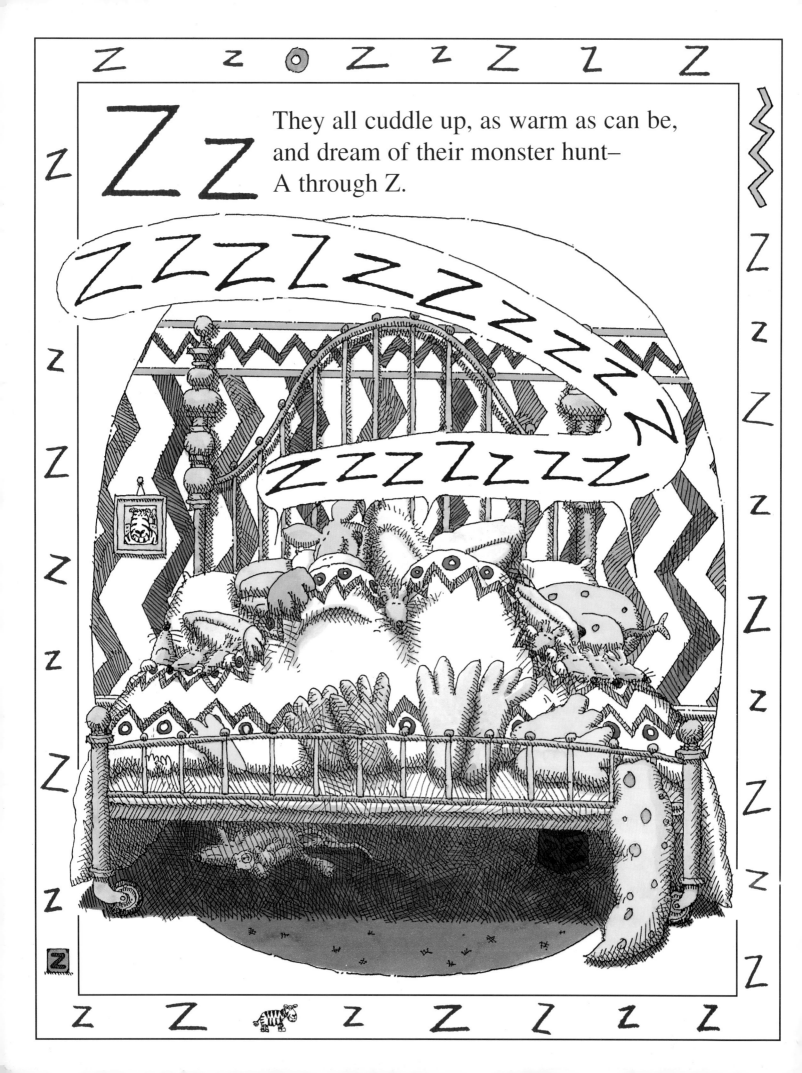

They all cuddle up, as warm as can be,
and dream of their monster hunt–
A through Z.

*Some of the less familiar animals and objects
featured in the art borders are:*

Emu	A large, flightless Australian bird
Harmonica	A small, rectangular wind instrument
Javelin	A slender shaft usually made of metal, thrown for distance in an athletic field event
Kimono	A loose robe with wide sleeves and a broad sash traditionally worn as an outer garment by the Japanese
X-ray fish	A tropical fish found in Venezuelan and Guyanese waters